Copyright 2016 @ Dr. Hitesh Sharma

All Rights Reserved

Thank you for downloading this eBook. This eBook remains the copyrighted property of Dr. Hitesh Sharma. You do not have the rights to reproduce, copy or distribute this book, either in complete or in part, for commercial or non-commercial purposes.

Thank you for your support.

About the Author

My name is Dr. Hitesh Sharma and I am thirty one years of age. I lead an easy-going retired life, while being perfectly healthy, wealthy and happy.

To me retirement doesn't actually mean sitting at home. It is a stage where my life is in my control and I can live my life the way I want. I get to decide whether to work or not; and I have made sure things go on smoothly at work even during my absence. I have taken steps to make sure my money works for me and not the other way round. I have also made sure I am in the pink of health.

Born and brought up to a lower middle class family in a small village near Bharatpur, Rajasthan, India, I have worked my way to achieve what I have always dreamed of achieving – Successful Entrepreneurship.

About the Author

I worked for about six years in the software industry after having achieved a degree in BCA, MCA, followed by a PhD in Computer Science. It is only then that I bootstrapped my own software company in the year 2012. Today I own an export house and a couple of ecommerce businesses – all thriving.

It troubles me to see the Workaholics of today, who have no life apart from their work. They work round the clock and have no time to spend with their families and friends. Vacations are things that happen only in dreams. As a reward all that they gain are a couple of lifestyle ailments such as heart disease, diabetes, hypertension and backaches.

Although I am not really an author by profession, I take this opportunity to share with you the 12 secrets that can lead you towards a life where you can retire young in a healthy, wealthy and happy way. These secrets have helped me immensely and I sincerely hope they will be of use to you too.

Acknowledgements

I was in class 12th in 2000 when I happened to flip through Robert T. Kiyosaki's Rich Dad Poor Dad. It completely changed my perspective towards wealth. Ever since then, Kiyosaki has been the No.1 role model in Life.

In 2012, I started my first business- a software company, called Digitize Software Pvt. Ltd. My partner Kishan was the first to spot the spark in me and he was the one who helped me through life's thick and thin. He inspired me enough to push harder for more, especially when those chips were down. This helped us grow and help our clients grow too.

Mark Shenton, the founder of Wool Overs Ltd. UK, was one of our first and foremost clients. The company runs knitwear ecommerce websites in UK, US and seven other countries. We gave our creative 100% to the site and Wool Overs went on to gather almost 1.5 million customers. I can't thank Mark enough for the trust that he placed in us.

Further, I would like to thank the incredible team at Digitize Software Pvt. Ltd and tapestry ecommerce. I cannot forget to thank the team of our export brand, Bless International™, which has helped us manage the Amazon US store "Bless Jewels" and Amazon UK store "Bless World" with 100% positive reviews, over these years.

Acknowledgements

On a more personal note, I would also like to thank my parents who have been a constant source of inspiration for me. They were the ones who kept reminding me that good health should be my top priority in life. At the age of 66, both my parents are more fit when compared to many youngsters who have succumbed to problems such as backaches, diabetes and hyper-tension because of their sedentary life-styles.

A very special thanks to the two angels in my life, my wife Archana and my daughter Ritvi, who have brought an exceptional stroke of love and luck, without which my life would have been incomplete.

Finally, I would like to thank my editor, Nanditha, who has helped me write this book. This book would not have been possible without her support.

-Dr. Hitesh Sharma

Note to My Readers

The main purpose behind writing this book is to change the perspective of my readers towards health, wealth and happiness. This will benefit everyone who is struggling with wealth, health or both issues.

I would like to share my personal email id at the end of this book, so you can dash off your emails to me. I promise to send out a prompt reply to each one of you.

I hope, reading this book brings in as much meaning into your lives, as writing the same has brought into my life.

Preface

Our parents have always told us to study well and work towards getting a good job. Is that all life is? Will that lead to a life that is full of happiness, health and wealth? I don't think so!

We work hard all our lives to make ends meet. We try to satisfy all the requirements of our family members. We compromise on those vacations that we so deserve in life. As a reward we get ailments and illnesses that take off all our savings. There is hardly anything left for our future. We end up financially depending upon our children for our day-to-day needs and maybe healthcare expenses too. Is that the kind of life we have dreamt for ourselves? I am sure you would say no.

All of us have dreams and we all want those dreams to come true. But how many of us actually work towards it? Just a handful! This is why there are just a few successful entrepreneurs while the others just lead an average working life.

Preface

This book is about dreaming big, about training your mind to succeed, about setting your priorities right, about exploring your options and about finding fulfillment in what you do. It finally takes you towards a life full of happiness, health and wealth, while giving you an option to retire while you are still young.

So, as you read this book, be prepared to pay the price for living a life that you deserve:

A life full of possibilities....

A life with no regrets....

A life that you can create all by yourself....

This book will take you on a journey to meet a young man, who faltered, made mistakes, but eventually had the foresight to learn from those mistakes. He is today a healthier, fitter and remarkably successful person in his chosen profession.

Preface

He chooses whether he wants to work or not. He lives life according to his terms. In case you are wondering who I am talking about, it is me!

Being Semi-autobiographical, it does not matter whether some of the anecdotes that I share with you in this book are real or apocryphal. What matters are the lessons I learnt, and the secrets that I would like to share with you through this book.

With simple parables, real life anecdotes, powerful visualization techniques, to-do-exercises, homework sheets, memory aides, and a semi-fictionalized story of an ordinary man finding his destiny in an extraordinary life, you may find my journey exciting - but better still - through my journey you may also get a glimpse into your own life.

Flip through the pages of the book and when you finally put it down, I guarantee, you will be a more reflective person, nay a changed person, altogether.

Table of Contents

About the Author 1

Acknowledgements 3

Note to My Readers 5

Preface 6

Introduction 10

Secret #1: Dream Big 20

Secret #2: Make Your Mind Your Best Friend 24

Secret #03: Be Happy First; Success will Follow 32

Secret #04: Train your Mind to Succeed 38

Secret #05: Relax and then Focus 56

Secret #06: Health is More Important than Success or Wealth 61

Secret #07: Use it or Lose it! 76

Secret #08: Be Different; you don't have to follow the Crowd 86

Secret #09: Explore your Options before you Jump 98

Secret #10: Find Fulfilment in your Life and Work 105

Secret #11: Live in Tune with Your True Self 118

Secret #12: Retire While you are Still Young 136

Promise yourself . . .

*To be so strong that
nothing can disturb your peace of mind.*

*To talk health, happiness and prosperity
to every person you meet.*

*To look at the sunny side of everything
and make your optimism come true*

*To think only of the best, to work
only for the best and to expect only the best*

*To be too large for worry,
too noble for anger, too strong for fear,
and too happy to permit the presence of trouble*

Introduction

Often people who work the hardest are the ones that struggle for money. However, this does not make them successful. Even if they do achieve success it will be at the cost of their health and happiness.

As Bill Gates said,

> ***"If you're born poor it is not your mistake; but if you die poor, it is your mistake"***

Many of us are born poor; so was I. However, this didn't stop me from dreaming of becoming a successful entrepreneur. Once the dream was there I also found the way to achieve it by grabbing on to the opportunities that came my way.

I was an average employee in the software industry for six years of my life; but I took this phase as a stepping stone to start my own software company in 2012. Most of my colleagues are still there, working hard to make ends meet. And here I am, at the age of 31, retired, healthy, wealthy and happy.

Making money is only the first step in achieving a Happy and Fulfilled Life. The most important step is to make your money work for you, without you getting into the financial struggle. The faster you achieve this, the earlier you can retire and start enjoying life.

Introduction

Meanwhile you will also have to pay close attention to your health and your lifestyle. Getting up early, working out, sticking on to a healthy diet and adopting an active lifestyle are all steps you need to take, to achieve and maintain perfect health. It is definitely easier said than done.

A determination to retire young, healthy, wealthy and happy is what you would need, to get there. If you have it in you, this book can be of great help to you. I have revealed in this book, 12 Secrets that have helped me achieve whatever I have ever dreamed about in life. I sincerely hope these secrets will help you look at life from a different perspective and show you the way to retire young, in a healthy, wealthy and happy way.

Here is a Sneak Peek into what you are getting into, by reading this book:

Secret #1

The first secret is about dreaming big. The logic is very simple. If you want to achieve something big, you will have to dream big. A dream is something that will give you a purpose in life. This will tell you where you want to go. If not, there is simply no point in living.

Introduction

A big dream gives you all the confidence that you need, while raising your self-esteem and self-image. It will inspire you to carve out a road map that you will follow step by step, to reach where you want to be. If people aren't laughing at your dreams, then they aren't big enough!

Secret #2

Once you have a dream, you may need a friend who will help you achieve this dream. Look no further. Your Mind can become your best friend. So, the second secret is all about making your mind, your best friend. To transform your dream into reality, all you need to do is tap into your personal power to overcome obstacles and create your destiny.

There is a need to strike a balance between your personal and professional life and between health and wealth, to gain happiness, fulfillment and Bliss. It is all about having a positive outlook, throwing out negatives, building your immune system and painting your days bright

Secret #3

Secret number 3 emphasizes the importance of being happy in order to achieve success. The definitions of success and happiness differ from person to person; but once you define these, it becomes easier to set your priorities right. It is all about defining your goals clearly, prioritizing them, identifying obstacles, affirming your goal and starting to work towards the same.

Secret #4

The fourth secret is about training your mind to succeed. By mind, I refer to the conscious as well as the subconscious parts of your mind. You will have to train both parts of your mind to sync and work together towards achieving your objective. It is all about delivering the right message to your subconscious mind frequently, so that eventually it becomes your driving force during each sleeping and waking moment of your life. The chapter describes all the techniques and strategies you can use, to train your mind to succeed.

Secret #5

This talks about the importance of being in a relaxed state of mind, in order to be able to focus on life, in a better way. In such a state,

Introduction

it becomes very easy to reprogram your super computer, which is your mind. It is your subconscious mind that takes charge when you are in this state. Any change in habit, behavior or attitude that your conscious mind desires can easily be accomplished while you are in this state. This chapter helps you in attaining this state of mind using various proven methods.

Secret #6

In the rat race of life where you run behind gaining wealth and success, health usually ends up taking a back step. This can have serious repercussions on your life. Therefore, this secret is all about prioritizing your health. In very simple ways, this chapter teaches you how to change your lifestyle, adopt a healthy diet and detoxify your body to achieve and maintain a perfect state of health.

Secret #7

This Secret is named 'Use it or Lose it.' It stresses on the importance of maintenance which is very essential whether it is your health, wealth, habits, talents, brains or those muscles that you have taken so much of your time and efforts, to develop. If you don't use them you end up losing them.

Introduction

In the form of a few easy tips, this chapter helps you in developing good habits that are necessary to achieve a healthy, wealthy and happy life forever.

Secret #8

Being an average human being may not require much from your side. You can just follow what everyone else is doing. However, if you want to achieve success in life by pursuing some special or extra ordinary talents you might have, it is necessary to be different from the crowd. This is exactly what this secret is about. It talks about how entrepreneurs are different from the crowd and what are the things that can stop you from being different from the crowd.

However, it also touches on the negative side of going away from the crowd – the loneliness and the separation from the herd. Yet, you get to receive one of the greatest rewards for believing in yourself - Happiness, Success and lots of money!

Introduction

Secret #9

When you are following the herd, your options are usually restricted. However, once you decide to get away from the herd mentality, your options become limitless. You can explore any or even a couple of these options until you end up with one that would be absolutely perfect for you. This chapter is about assessing yourself, finding your interests and focusing on your future, as that is where you are going to be for the rest of your life.

Secret #10

This secret is probably the most important of all. It talks about finding fulfillment in your life and work. It is about living in the moment and putting your heart, soul and mind into whatever you do. With simple steps that you can adopt in your daily life, this chapter teaches you how to achieve the highest fulfillment in your life.

Secret #11

Living in tune with yourself is what this secret teaches you. It is about aligning your inner-self with your outer-self and achieving the peace of mind that is crucial for retiring young, healthy, wealthy and happy. This chapter gives you a few simple tips to follow that can take you a long way in achieving your goal in a stress-free and relaxed way.

It also talks about reconnecting with your passions and playing to your talents which can help you live much more in tune with yourself.

Secret #12

Most of us wish to work till we drop. However, we do not realize that this is not the right way to live for when you retire sick and tired, there is no way you can enjoy life. This secret is about helping you retire while you are still young, hale and healthy. While giving a brief insight into my life, this chapter talks about changing your outlook and your lifestyle the way many young retirees did. This can change your perspective about life and get you on the road to retire young, healthy, wealthy and happy.

Introduction

This book is all about empowering you with the necessary knowledge that you would need, to pursue your dreams and achieve a healthy, wealthy and happy retired life. For a detailed version on how to get rid of your financial hardships and retire early in a healthy and wealthy way, await my next book….

'How I retired at 31, healthy and wealthy.'

Till then, Happy Reading!

Secret #1: Dream Big

> *"There are dreams to be dreamed, there are ventures to be started, and there are new songs to be sung - when you have hope in your heart."*

Have you seen the latest work of DreamWorks Animation called Turbo? It is about how a small snail could race in the Indianapolis 500. The film sends home an excellent message —"no dream is too big and no dreamer is too small."

When I was a child, I was taught in school that I must always look at the sunnier side of a story. If you want the moon, you have to literally stand on tip-toe and imagine it's falling into your outstretched palm and you are grabbing it. I remember doing that so often because I wanted to be an astronaut when I grew up.

It's another story altogether that when I got into college, my dream changed into something else. When I read Robert Kiyosaki's much acclaimed *Rich Dad Poor Dad*, I found my purpose in life. I knew I wanted to be an Entrepreneur.

Secret #1: Dream Big

Always dream big because if you dream small, you will accomplish only a few things in life. Your life would remain mediocre. We teach our children about renunciation. We don't give them dreams of wealth creation and wealth distribution. If you don't have the resources yourself, can you even be of any help to others?

Only the powerful - the rich and the able like Bill Gates and Warren Buffett can aim to be philanthropists. Paupers cannot be philanthropists. The size of your dreams will determine where you will end up. So don't be a miser when it comes to dreaming.

When you dream big, your self-esteem and self-confidence rises. Your self-image improves. The reason so many people accomplish so little is because they never allow themselves to dream big, imagine the impossible or claim the kind of life that they secretly dream for themselves.

Secret #1: Dream Big

As early as in 1976, when Steve Jobs and his high school pal, Steve Wozniak, were assembling circuit boards in a garage owned by Jobs at his parents' house in Los Altos, California, Jobs had a vision to "put a computer in the hands of everyday people."

Did he realize that dream?

Sure he did, even after once being ousted from the company he had so zealously founded.

Likewise, in 1961, John F. Kennedy told his country folks, "This nation should commit itself, before this decade is out, of landing a man on the moon and returning him safely to earth." Listener's thought Kennedy had set an impossible deadline. However, three men did land on the moon ahead of their President's set deadline.

If you, as a child, have read *Alice in Wonderland*, you would recall this sequence:

One day, Alice came to a fork in the road and saw a Cheshire cat sitting on a tree. The conversation went like this:

Secret #1: Dream Big

Alice: "Which road do I take?"

Cat: "Where do you want to go?"

Alice:" I don't know."

Cat: "Then it doesn't matter!"

Moral of the story: You should know where you want to go! A dream, big or small, cannot materialize on its own if you don't have a road map in your hand. The day you put your dream in black and white before you, would be the day it would begin to realize, piece by piece and cell by cell.

This formula worked for me, and I am sure it will work for you too.

Secret #2: Make Your Mind Your Best Friend

If you think you are beaten you are;
If you think you dare not, you don't;
If you want to win but think you can't;
It's almost a cinch you won't.

If you think you'll lose you're lost;
For out of the world we find
Success begins with a fellow's will;
It's all in a state of mind.

Life's battles don't always go
To the stronger and faster man,
But sooner or later the man who wins
Is the man who thinks he can.

Secret #2: Make Your Mind Your Best Friend

In college, I once knew a boy, who also hailed from a modest family like I did. However, he had a terrific gift of visualization.

He wanted to take up the UPSC (Union Public Service Commission) exam and become an IAS officer, which is the ultimate dream of the upwardly mobile youth in India. When I met him, he had been preparing for UPSC for almost four years. Till then he had not given up on his dreams.

In the interim, I could complete my BCA (Bachelor of Computer Application) and the second semester of MCA (Master of Computer Application), while he was still stuck in the hot pursuit of his dream. Once during a time of idle bantering, I picked up the courage to ask him about the four years of his life that he had invested in his dream, without making any substantial progress, while I had already chalked out a definite career path for myself. "Aren't you afraid that if you don't get selected again, all your time and efforts would go waste?"

In reply, he smiled and said, "Hitesh, it does scare me at times. But whenever I am in doubt or fear, I shut my eyes and visualize the hawker, who comes to drop the newspaper at my room.

Next, I imagine picking up the newspaper and seeing my name splashed on the front page as the topper on the UPSC list - above One million other aspirants!"

This man (whose identity I wish to hold back) was so completely focused on the end outcome; so determined to make this dream come true that when he recounted this vision to me he had a 100-watt smile flashing on his face.

Any surprise that with that kind of unwavering conviction, he did eventually top the exam and is now posted as a civil servant and enjoying the life he dreamed of.

Very often, you would have noticed that you and your friend down the street may have attended the same school, gone to the same college, had the same set of teachers, attended the same business management program and learnt the same techniques; yet one goes on to be hugely successful in his career, while the other continues to struggle the rest of his life.

This happens because the one who succeeds knows the secret to personal success. He is not smarter, better or brighter than you are. He has just mastered the trick to tap into his personal power to overcome hurdles and create his own destiny. He knows how to turn dreams into reality, create meaningful relationships, and always be at a peak-performance state.

Secret #2: Make Your Mind Your Best Friend

I did not learn this secret in a day or two. In fact, I also made many blunders, was distracted in my studies, even failed my BCA 1st year examinations and was considered as one of the mediocre students. Until one day it got me thinking: What's the missing element in my life?

And gradually it began to dawn on me that something was amiss. Being the topper in class may not be the right definition of success; but being a topper in life most certainly is. Successful entrepreneurs' biographies told me that most 'Grade A' students end up working for 'Grade C' students.

Harrison Ford was illiterate and Thomas Alwa Edison attended school only till Grade Four. Bill Gates is another oft-cited example of a famous Harvard dropout. I realized that what was missing in my life - Balance. I had to find that perfect balance in my life - balance between wealth and health; between my personal and professional life.

Ranjan Das, the CEO of SAP-Indian Subcontinent, died young from a massive heart attack. Doctors pinned the blame on insomnia or lack of sleep. Das used to sleep only for four to five hours in a day. He could not strike a balance between the demands of his personal and professional life.

Here is a story that I would like to share with you. I hope you find it as inspiring as I did.

Two seeds got flung on to a fertile ground.

The first seed quipped, "I want to grow tall! I want to have my roots deep down into the soil. I want to spread my leaves far and wide. I want to produce beautiful flowers and fruits. I want to feel the warmth of the sun, the moistness of the soil, the nutrients coursing through my veins and the brilliant shine of the morning dew falling on my flowers."

And so she grew as tall and as mighty as she had imagined.

Secret #2: Make Your Mind Your Best Friend

The second seed mumbled, "If I send my roots too deep into the ground, the little insects in the soil may nibble on them. If I grow too tall, the harsh lights of the sun may burn my soft leaves. If I let my buds open, crawlers might creep into them, and children may pluck and destroy my beautiful blossoms."

So this seed waited and wished nothing.

Guess what happened.

In the morning the gardener came and swept this seed away.

The plucky one held its ground, clunk fast to its beliefs and one day managed to grow into a tall tree.

I remember whenever we had trouble at home, instead of fretting, raving or ranting, my mother would say, "Aren't we all lucky?"

We didn't understand the significance of that statement then. But today I do. What she meant was that things could be worse, but weren't, because we had the potential to deal with those challenges. With that kind of belief, life did not appear so full of hardships.

As a Computer Science student I discovered that our mind is also a super computer. It can be programmed any which way you want. You can choose what software program to install, remove the one that is not working and with those simple changes, change the world around you. You have control over the programming. Whatever you put into it is reflected in what comes out.

Like that little seed, we all have two choices in life - Yes and No.

Do you want...

- ☑ *Success?*
- ☑ *Money?*
- ☑ *A good physique and a healthy body?*
- ☑ *More wealth?*
- ☑ *A positive attitude?*
- ☑ *Fulfilling relationships?*

Secret #2: Make Your Mind Your Best Friend

Then all you need to do is program your mind, accordingly.

Having a positive outlook in life reflects the 'yes' choice. You can choose to think thoughts that build up your self-confidence, throw all negativity out of your life, build your immune system and paint your days bright with a heavy dose of optimism.

*I promise you that with these small changes, all worries and obstacles in your life **will begin to dissipate - in no time!***

Just try it!

Secret #03: Be Happy First; Success will Follow

> *Success is being right; happiness is being true.*
>
> *Success is earned; happiness is achieved.*
>
> *Success is awards; happiness is its own reward.*
>
> *Success is pursuing your dreams;*
>
> *happiness is living your dreams.*
>
> *Success is reaching the top; happiness has no ceiling.*
>
> *Success is just ahead; happiness was never behind.*
>
> *Success is pursued; happiness is acquired.*

Most people think that happiness comes from success and vice versa. But that's a mistaken belief. Happiness may not always follow success, although happy people are generally always successful. This is because they radiate positive vibes and attract all positive vibes to them.

Success is something most of us want; but do we all also want happiness?

Secret #03: Be Happy First; Success will Follow

I don't think so. That's why most successful and wealthy people are not always the happiest ones. I think they have got their priorities wrong.

Wang Junyao, the chairman of Junyao Group, was 38 when he died of cancer, caused by high pressure, anxiety and a life packed with so many things. He may have been very successful; but was he happy? I doubt it very much.

How you choose to personally define success or happiness is entirely up to you; but you can set your priorities right by recognizing the difference between the two.

Success comes from self-affirmation. It comes from the staunch belief that you deserve all the good things that are coming to you because you have worked hard for those rewards. On the other hand, if you are contented and complacent about what you have, how can you ever hope to achieve more in life?

I tried this on myself

I started applying my beliefs to change my small habits first.

When I was in college, I started waking up early, joined a gym, set a disciplined routine for myself, shunned non-productive distractions and instead picked up the habit of reading good literature.

I started reading for fun and learning and not just to pass an exam. I started to work on my body, started running, began to eat natural, healthy and wholesome food so that I could develop immunity against all kinds of infections and diseases.

My life started changing. Instead of dreading what lay ahead, I would wake up feeling excited and cheerful to start my day.

Then a strange thing happened

My happiness led to improved efficiency. I became smarter in class. I was putting in fewer hours, but getting more work and study done. My memory and retention power started improving. My mind felt clear and fully charged-up.

Stress was no longer a part of my life. Problems that once seemed big and insurmountable now appeared smaller and easier to overcome. And with my healthy mind, body and soul, I became more focused on achieving the success, I knew I deserved.

Elementary, isn't it?

The Process of Setting Goals

Follow these tips on setting goals, and you will never go off the mark:

- Define Goals
- Prioritize Them
- Identify Obstacles
- Affirm Objectives

(A) DEFINE your goals in clear, unambiguous terms, e.g., I want to make X amount of money today.

(B) PRIORITIZE and re-prioritise your goals. This will help you make the best use of your time, so that no important goal gets less of your attention.

(C) IDENTIFY your obstacles. These could be internal as well as external. Decide what additional skills or knowledge you would need, to achieve your goals.

(D) AFFIRM your goal and start working towards it. Merely repeating: "How can I create a more positive impression on my boss today?" will set you on a correctional course.

Now just run for your goal.

A few other tips...

- ☑ Write your goals in black and white.

- ☑ Set a concrete deadline for realizing each goal, e.g. "I am going to lose 10Kg by 3rd of November 2016," or "I will earn USD 100K per month by Jan 2017."

- ☑ Put the list in front of your bed so you continue to get inspired by it

- ☑ Gradually start weeding out all the negative thoughts from your mind and focus on building only positive energy.

- ☑ Lastly, get your subconscious mind, the most powerful reservoir of energy to work on your goals.

We'll learn more of these tricks in the subsequent sections of this book.

Secret #03: Be Happy First; Success will Follow

Life is good!

And you deserve it.

The question is not, "Who am I?" but rather, "Whom do I have the freedom to be?"

As you walk down the road to claim your success, understand that you need to get there mentally first, before you can get there physically!

Remember - you get only one life and there is no possibility of second chances. Make the most of this life NOW!

It doesn't matter how old you are, what you did, how qualified or unqualified you are, and whether or not you were born rich. What matters is that you have everything going for you, despite the odds in your life.

To put it simply: Go! Seek joy, look for fulfillment, dream big and pursue your dreams with all you have got!

Leave the rest either to your brain or to God's will because both will work and produce results.

Secret #04: Train your Mind to Succeed

A mental picture is worth a thousand words

Your subconscious will begin to work on
any picture that is backed by a strong faith.

Imagine the end and
feel believe that it's already a reality.

Follow it through, and
you will get the outcome you desire.

Live the joy and peace you
seek in realizing your most cherished goals.

Scientifically apply this principle,
until you prove to yourself that every thought will
produce an action, when you slip it into your
subconscious
mind that will finally turn it into conscious thinking.

Secret #04: Train your Mind to Succeed

Like the hidden portion of an iceberg, our subconscious comprises of about 80% of our mind. The remaining 20% belongs to the conscious!! Yes, we continue to ignore and grossly under-utilize the immense power of this subconscious mind.

You would have heard your teachers, parents and other influencers constantly say "remember to do this," "pay attention to that" "concentrate" etc.

But did they ever tell you, "Slip this thought into your subconscious mind and let it tap into that hidden reservoir of energy?

Because we so completely and conveniently ignore the power of the subconscious mind that resides within us, we often don't know how to apply it to our advantage.

However your subconscious, involuntary mind is more powerful than you can imagine. Put it to good use and it can change the entire landscape of your life, making you the master controller of your destiny.

Secret #04: Train your Mind to Succeed

Mind power is about directing both your conscious and your subconscious mind to work in sync for the same objective. Whatever your conscious mind desires, your subconscious mind can achieve. You just have to keep delivering the right message to your subconscious mind at right intervals and frequently, so that eventually it becomes your driving force during each sleeping and waking moment of your life.

Thomas Edison once observed, "Ideas come from space." This may be a little hard to believe; but often the most creative ideas do appear to spring up from seemingly nowhere.

Secret #04: Train your Mind to Succeed

Archimedes found the key to the principle of buoyancy during a bath.

Elias Howe, the inventor of the sewing machine, saw the design flash in his dream. In his own words, "I saw in my dream that I was in Africa chased by a pack of cannibals (A tribe of primitive human beings who feed on other human beings' flesh). They caught me and placed me in a huge pot. I kept trying to get out but they kept pushing me back into the broth with sharp-edged spears." These spears had holes at the tips - and that gave him the inspiration he was so desperately looking for!

Our subconscious mind is a primitive reservoir of all our memory, fears, phobias, behavioral patterns, habits, beliefs, and expectations.

A scientific fact is that only 2-4% of our day is controlled by our conscious mind.

The rest (96-98%) is controlled by the subconscious.

It beats our heart, digests our food, and breathes for us all, without us making any conscious effort to control these activities. If that were not the case, imagine how little a time we would have, to carry out all our routine chores. We'd go absolutely crazy.

Secret #04: Train your Mind to Succeed

Do you know where the world's most celebrated artists, innovators, poets, painters, scientists etc., get their ideas from? Is it because of their knowledge, hard work, maybe a lucky break or God's gift? Or is something else at work here?

Since it's that section of your brain that is always "on," you can tap into its power anytime, whether you are awake or fast asleep. If you make a conscious effort, it can tune into your inner processes, your articulated or unarticulated dreams and work on it, even without your conscious effort. Therefore, when you are nurturing a specific goal or a dream, consciously repeat to yourself...

> "I believe in the power of my subconscious mind.
>
> It will make me realize all my dreams and desires."

I recall using this technique so many times, during my days in college, whenever I felt down in the dumps and believe me, every time it worked!

Secret #04: Train your Mind to Succeed

I read somewhere that Walt Disney had his own unusual method of coming up with powerful ideas. Whenever a brain wave struck him, Disney would run it through a meticulous three-step process to ensure that his idea always turned out to be innovative, powerful and practical.

Unlike today's product engineers who are armed with MBA degrees, he did not analyze market conditions.

He did not study rival products.

He did not set a budget.

He would simply shut his eyes, and dream.

All my college years, I remember doing the same, and invariably it worked!

People who succeed in life, despite the presence of so many odds, share one thing in common: They tap into the force beyond the conscious boundaries of their minds, and draw from it, infinite amounts of wisdom, inspiration and success.

Can you not do something similar and reap rich rewards?

Winston Churchill, one of the greatest statesmen the world has ever known, was once invited to address the graduating class at Harrow, the school he had attended several years ago. It was the beginning of World War II when Churchill was the prime minister of England. On the morning of his address, the small auditorium was filled chock-a-block with some of the brightest, young minds of the school. All were eager to hang on to every spoken word of Churchill.

When Churchill took the podium and glanced around to take in the jam-packed audience, his thoughts flew back to his own school days, when he would sit behind one of those wooden desks. With this in mind, he muttered the most inspiring words to a packed audience of impressionable minds,

> *"Never give in---never, never, never, never,*
>
> *in nothing great or small, large or petty.*
>
> *Never give in except to convictions of*
>
> *honor and good sense.*
>
> *Never yield to force.*
>
> *Never yield to the apparently overwhelming*
>
> *might of the enemy."*

What powerful oratory!

That fateful day, Churchill managed to convince his audience that their minds are their most powerful weapons against all odds in life. Your belief system can change the way you perceive the world and arm you with all the ammunition to gun for the ultimate.

Secret #04: Train your Mind to Succeed

Thomas Edison, after he had invented the light bulb, admitted that he had tried over a thousand times to make the invention work. A curious bystander asked "What kept you going after so many failures?" and Edison shook his head vigorously in denial and said, "Young man, I did not fail. I merely discovered a thousand ways of how NOT to make an electric bulb."

That's what kept him going - his unshakable belief in his power to invent. Edison must have discreetly slipped this thought into his subconscious mind and it began to work on it.

Most smokers know that their habit can lead them to lung cancer. Yet they choose to bellow smoke from their nostrils like human chimneys, because they don't believe in their power to auto-correct their self-destructive behavior.

People are aware that fat people can't walk properly, nor look their best and develop early health problems; yet they can't stop binging.

There's clearly no lack of consciousness in these people; yet they embark on the path to self-destruction. If only, they'd somehow rope in their subconscious minds, they might be able to amend their behavior and be in better charge of their health.

Secret #04: Train your Mind to Succeed

The latest statistics indicate that fewer than one in five people who follow a formal weight loss program actually succeed in losing weight.

Isn't it clear why the failure rate is so high? Because despite all the New Year resolutions, the behavioral patterns of these people remain unchanged. They continue to produce the same undesirable results because they haven't re-conditioned their thoughts and behavioral patterns with the help of their subconscious minds.

During my programming days, we learnt that when the memory of a hard disc is full, you cannot upload more data into it. You would have to first delete some unwanted files, clean up the disc space, re-format if need be, and then store the new information. It's exactly the same way with our subconscious mind. You must wash out the old "success blocker programs" and install new "success enabler programs" on your hard disc.

How is this possible?

Very simple

Secret #04: Train your Mind to Succeed

Through the power of visualization

If you haven't watched the 2010 British historical *film 'The King's Speech"* directed by Tom Hooper, written by David Seidler, you may want to watch this trailer now https://www.youtube.com/watch?v=pzI4D6dyp_o.

I had tears stinging my eyes when I saw Colin Firth (playing a very vulnerable *King* George VI with a pronounced and highly debilitating stammer, especially for a King who has to make many public appearances and address his people) yell *"Because I have a voice!"* and his speech therapist Geoffrey Rush respond "*Yes you do!*"

Consciously or unconsciously, all peak performers, ace sportspersons, athletes, CEOs, top executives, talented movie stars, skilled doctors, surgeons, celebrated poets, singers and artists use the power of visualization to condition their minds for success for an important event/surgery/performance. Knowingly or unknowingly they practice their moves, speeches, their patterns etc., and keep on programming and re-programming their minds to succeed.

Secret #04: Train your Mind to Succeed

Sir Winston Churchill, who led Britain during World War II, was not in the best of health during his most influential days as a statesman. But his willpower was the reason he achieved success. "**Success is not final, failure is not fatal**: it is the courage to continue that counts." he once said. "We shall fight them on the beaches," he declared in one of his most famous speeches before leading his country to war.

If you want inspiration, watch Gabriele Muccino's Will Smith starrer 2006 film **The Pursuit of Happiness. The movie is** based on Chris Gardner, a down-in-the-dumps salesman-turned stockbroker. The best sequence in the movie was Will Smith's straight talk with his little son.

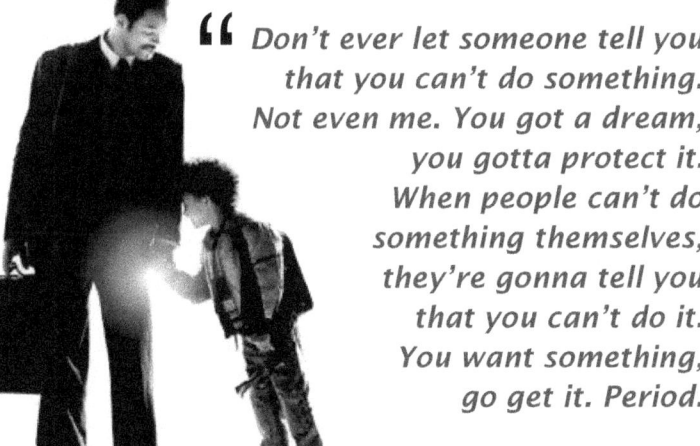

> *Don't ever let someone tell you that you can't do something. Not even me. You got a dream, you gotta protect it. When people can't do something themselves, they're gonna tell you that you can't do it. You want something, go get it. Period.*
>
> -Will Smith
> (The Pursuit of Happiness film)

Let's face it. Your mind is a super computer. If you have the perseverance and unshakable self-belief, it can literally manifest anything that you truly desire. Just remember that your subconscious mind cannot distinguish between the real and the imagined and that is indeed a good thing.

So all that you need to do is focus all your energies, your conscious thoughts, feelings, emotions and imagination on one or two clear objectives and sooner rather than later, they would begin to come true. This is a truly remarkable gift that each one of us is born with!

Visualization can be used to create some amazing results. Genius scientist Albert Einstein, who once said "Imagination is more important than knowledge," used visualization techniques all his life.

Auto Suggestion

Have you ever had to tell yourself - now breathe?

Now digest?

Now excrete?

Never Right?

Secret #04: Train your Mind to Succeed

This is because your mind is pre-programmed to carry out all these activities, even in the absence of any prompts from your conscious mind. Had that not been the case, you'd probably be dead meat by now. This is nature's way of de-stressing our mind.

However you can use this powerful tool of auto-suggestion to energize your conscious activities as well. The other name for auto-suggestions is positive affirmations. It's the simplest and undoubtedly, one of the most powerful mind programming tools available to us, free-of-cost. Best news is that this tool is accessible anywhere and anytime, even when you are on the go, in office, at work, anywhere. It's the most effective tool used in Psychotherapy and alternative medicine, to promote self-healing, self-empowerment and self-esteem.

All you have to do is design and create your own autosuggestion statements for the situation that you want to deal with. You can then harness all 18 billion brain cells to work for you in sync for a particular goal.

For starters, tell yourself:
I am a beautiful creation

Secret #04: Train your Mind to Succeed 53

I am super intelligent

- ☑ **I am confident and capable**
- ☑ **I am extremely intelligent and creative**
- ☑ **I am unlimited**
- ☑ **I attract people with my positive vibes**

Instant Confidence Builder
This exercise has been culled from Paul McKenna's
Instant Confidence:
The Power to Go For Anything You Want!

(1) Stand up and put your attention on your 'One Point' – about an inch below your navel and roughly halfway between your navel and your spine. This point is known in Japanese as 'hare', and is believed to be both the physical center of your body and the central storage point for your 'kid', 'chi', or life force. If it helps, place one hand over that area of your stomach – I find that I like keeping my thumb up across my navel as it works well for me. You may also like to visualize a ball of energy radiating from that spot.

(2) Now, think about a situation coming up in your life that you are worried or upset about. (This is not the time for major phobias – start with something relatively minor). If you have someone working with you, have them push you gently on the shoulder. You will find that you are very easily pushed off balance.

(3) Continue thinking about that difficult situation. Give your discomfort level a score from 1 (at peace) to 10 (Aaaargh!)

(4) Now bring you attention back to 'One Point'. Place your hand over that area of your stomach to help guide your mind. If you have someone working with you, have them once again push you gently on the shoulder. You will know you are at 'One Point' when it is very difficult for them to push you off balance.

(5) Finally, holding 'One Point' attention, think about the situation you were upset or worried about. Now notice the discomfort drain away from 10 (or wherever it was on the scale) down to 1. Again, if someone is working with you they can monitor your attention by pushing gently against your shoulder as you do this, to make sure you are holding 'One Point'.

Secret #04: Train your Mind to Succeed

(6) When you no longer feel any discomfort thinking about the situation, you can use your 'One Point' attention to mentally rehearse on performing your best. When you are actually in the situation, you can hold 'One Point' as you perform, to ensure you will stay centered and peaceful throughout.

Secret #05: Relax and then Focus

> *Your mind will answer most questions if you learn to relax and wait for the answer*
>
> -William S. Burroughs

Relaxation is the key to gain access to your subconscious mind

KhulJa SIM SIM!

When you get yourself into a relaxed, focused state (The alpha state in medical parlance) you are perfectly primed for reprogramming your super computer. This is when the first change happens. Your subconscious mind takes the driver's seat and the conscious mind, slips into the passenger seat. Though still present, this takes a backseat. In this position you are amenable to any change in your behavior, attitude or habit that your conscious mind desires.

When you relax, repeat

The only way to unlock that immense power of your subconscious mind is through perseverance!

Secret #05: Relax and then Focus

Relaxation puts you in a receptive mode - into a worthy receptacle into which nature can now pour its abundance. On the flip side, when you are stressed or burnt out, you are abruptly shifting your mind gears. You get distracted and you lose control over your vehicle. Metaphorically also, when the road is bumpy, you can't enjoy the drive. So melt away all the road blocks and gear up for a long, smooth ride.

In contrast, in a perfectly relaxed state, you are able to think straight, absorb more information, make better decisions and are far wiser. You are actually at your creative best.

To be happy, spread happiness

Have you ever heard of Heart Math? The Heart Math researchers have shown that our heart's rhythm and electrical signals change vastly with our emotions, and the most harmonious, perfect signals come when we feel (or even think of) positive emotions such as love, joy and appreciation. Such emotions create positive, infectious "vibes" around us that attract similar positive energies to us.

Secret #05: Relax and then Focus

Have you tried meditative prayer?

This is the process of spring cleaning. It happens when you clear out all the accumulated junk from your brain box and try to concentrate your energies on one particular thought, place, word, color or an object.

To meditate, you have to sit, kneel or lie down in a comfortable position and think about (or pray to) one specific entity or one specific thing. It may take upwards of ten minutes in order to completely clear your junkyard and fill it with one focused thought;

but that's normal for most people. This will take you deep into a heightened mental/spiritual state.

Secret #05: Relax and then Focus

Use the power of affirmations and self-talk to stay focused until you feel completely at peace and stress-free. It is now scientifically proven that meditation has many health benefits in addition to bringing about mental relaxation, lowering high blood pressure and reducing your high cholesterol as well as high blood sugar levels.

To get yourself into a meditative mood, play your favorite calming music - could be instrumental or a motivational upbeat number, or just a collection of powerful Vedic mantras, whose meaning you may or may not know. Just listening to them can recharge you. Try it with the most powerful Gayathri Mantra. Once relaxed, the rest will come easy.

You can create any future of your dreams merely by letting your subconscious mind take charge of your thoughts and beliefs. As God's creation, you are the most perfect human being. Imagine, see, believe, feel and then be the reality of what you want to be.

Begin to live that dream. Sustain and nourish it with a lot of love and imagination so that it eventually penetrates deep into your subconscious mind, until it becomes a firm conviction.

Secret #05: Relax and then Focus

The subconscious mind is a repository of all our painful and joyful memories. It retains every bit of detail from our past. Based on what you choose to pull out from this Pandora's Box – a happy or painful memory - you can create a glorious future for yourself.

Know that subconscious mind is super intelligent. It wants you to realize your true potential - you just have to ask for that help. If you are seeking a dream, believe that the dream is also seeking you. The very germ of success has the potential to make you succeed. Just as a small acorn has the potential to grow into a tall oak tree, your subconscious mind has the potential to transform your small dream into a big reality.

Repeat the word, "success," to yourself as frequently as you can and with full faith and conviction. Before you know it, you will succeed, exactly as you had dreamt of.

> "The best six doctors anywhere
>
> And no one can deny it
>
> Are sunshine, water, rest, air,
>
> Exercise and diet.
>
> These six will gladly you attend
>
> If only you are willing
>
> Your mind they'll ease
>
> Your will they'll mend
>
> And charge you not a shilling."

Good Health = Good Wealth

When Health is absent, wisdom cannot reveal itself, art cannot manifest, strength cannot fight, Wealth becomes useless, and intelligence cannot be applied.

- Herophilus

To me, Health implies Wealth and vice versa.

There is a rat race out there to gain Wealth and success. Most of us seem to take part in this race, without giving much thought to our Health. In the process, we lose our Health. If at all we do win this race and manage to gain success and Wealth, the failing Health does not allow us to enjoy those gains - ever.

Here's a story that explains this complex relationship between Health, Wealth and Success:

A woman happened to see three men who were seated in her front yard, when she came out of her house. They were old and had white, flowing beards. It was the first time she'd seen them.

She addressed them by saying, "I don't recognize anyone of you. However, I guess you must be hungry. If you can come inside my house, I will give you something to eat."

Secret #06: Health is More Important than Success or Wealth

Appreciating her concern, they asked her if her husband was at home to which she answered with a no.

Then they said "We cannot enter your house until the man of the house comes back. When her husband came back home in the evening, she narrated the incident to him and he said, "Let them know that I have come back home and invite them again."

When the woman went out of the house, she found them in the same place. She told them what her husband had told her and invited them inside. However, once again they declined to come. This time, when the woman asked the reason, one of them explained the situation to her.

He introduced one of his friends as Wealth, the other as Success and himself as Health. He then asked her to go inside and check with her husband which one of them they would like to invite home.

The husband was very happy to hear this. He said it would be very nice if they could invite Wealth and ask him to fill their home with Wealth. His wife's wish however was to invite Success. The daughter-in-law was listening to this conversation from a corner. She approached them and suggested that they invite Health, as that would fill their lives with joy.

Finally the husband and wife went ahead with their daughter-in-law's suggestion and invited Health to be their guest.

As Health accepted their invitation and started walking towards their house, the other two also joined him. Surprised to see this, the woman asked Success and Wealth, "How come you decided to join us when the invitation was only for Health?"

To this, Wealth and Success replied, "In case you had invited one of us, the other two would have stayed out. However, because you decided to invite Health we come along because….

Wherever there is Health, there will be Success and Wealth

If you ask me, I would say you will need all the three if you want to lead a happy life. It is true that Wealth and Success come with Health; but if you run after Health and work out at the gym all the time to build those 6-pack abs, you will not be left with enough time on your hands, to gain Wealth. Would you?

Secret #06: Health is More Important than Success or Wealth

In this material world, Wealth is something that all of us need. However, the reasons for seeking Wealth may differ from person to person. There are some who seek Wealth only to feel Wealthy and powerful. Then there are others for whom Wealth is mainly a means to discharge their responsibilities towards their families. While some need Wealth to clear off past debts, others may need it to travel the world. Unfortunately, there are many who need Wealth to be cured of their chronic illnesses that are the price they have paid, for being workaholics.

Do you fall in this last category of people?

I hope not, because if you do, then you are not really enjoying the fruits of your labor. You are spending all the money that you earn on surgeries, medicines and a battery of pathological tests.

You may not be allowed to eat all that you like.....

You may not be able to travel to those exotic destinations, even if you may have the motive and the means....

You may even have cut down on those fun-filled activities that you have always craved for.....

Secret #06: Health is More Important than Success or Wealth

No matter how much money you make, it is impossible to buy good Health. This is true even if that money can help you afford the best of the medical services and supplies available, in the world.

I have often seen that people, who resort to self-defeating and unhealthy lifestyles, keep struggling for Wealth in their lives. Your approach towards yourself affects your approach towards your work. A person who is careless and tardy about his Health would be inefficient and shoddy at work too. A dull mind cannot usually come up with brilliant ideas.

It's not just great Health that can lead to great Wealth. Your Wealth would mean absolutely nothing to you if you do not keep good Health. There is a very simple formula you need to follow, if you want to lead a Healthy life:

Healthy Life = Wholesome, Fresh & Natural Food + Exercise + Work/Life Balance

Secret #06: Health is More Important than Success or Wealth

Make it a point….

- ☑ To have some family or 'me' time everyday
- ☑ Not to worry too much about the mundane things of life
- ☑ To find peace within you and be content with what you have
- ☑ To accept things as they are and go with the flow

If life throws a Lemon at you, make some Lemonade out of it!

It is as simple as that!

Add the sugar of positive attitude in that lemon juice and enjoy your life, moment by moment.

Every seven years, our body changes completely. Each and every old cell gets replaced by new ones. But this process begins to slow down in mid-years. After that, what sustains us is good food, regular exercise and a positive mindset.

Do You Believe in Longevity Diet?

I do. Medical research indicates that certain communities seem to live longer than others. Have you ever wondered why? This is because of their diet patterns and food habits.

For instance, there is a place called Ryukyu Islands, off the Japanese coastline, where lives a tribe called Okinawa. Their diet consists mainly of yellow and green vegetables. An indigenous purple-fleshed sweet potato is their staple food. Compared to the Japanese diet that consists of a lot of rice, the Okinawan diet is 15% less grains and 30% less sugar with very little rice. The average life expectancy of these people is 81 years, while that of the people in United States is 78 and the rest of the world 67. Also, these people reportedly do not suffer from any major lifestyle diseases. Only nine out of every 100,000 are reported to ever develop heart diseases in Okinawa.

Secret #06: Health is More Important than Success or Wealth

It is their plant-based diet that is well-balanced and gives them lots of energy to withstand the risks of cancer, diabetes, hypertension and heart diseases.

You Are What You Eat

Does your car insurer give you 'no claim' bonus and charges lower premium for the year you drive your vehicle safely and meet with no accidents?

It's the same with your health.

Thanks to eating healthy; I've always paid smaller premiums on my medical insurance. This is because I watch my borderline hypertension and my lipid profile is better than average. My weight is a comfortable 75 kilos for my frame of 5' 11". I am not on any prescription drugs. That translates into lower insurance rates!

Staying healthy is a sure-shot way of saving on healthcare costs. This in turn is a sure-shot way of ensuring financial security at the time of your retirement.

My paternal aunt was 62, when my uncle's stroke changed her life forever. From enjoying her new role as a grandmother, she was juggling hospital visits, wheelchairs and sessions with occupational therapists.

How did this happen?

My uncle was a heavy drinker and a chain smoker. In the end, it's not just he, but others in the family too, who ended up paying a high cost of his poor lifestyle choices.

"You are what you eat"

Most of us have heard this adage; but do we really follow it?

We get tempted by junk food and give in; and when we do, we don't even keep track of how much we are eating. It's so seductive. Food cravings can seriously impair our capacity to think straight, focus, act appropriate and succeed.

There is a simple solution to this. If you cannot stop indulging yourself once in a while, try to avoid food that is rich in calories, the next day. This will help your body cleanse itself of the toxins that you loaded into it, the previous night.

Detoxification

It's a process through which you can cleanse your blood and eliminate all toxins from your body. This process eliminates toxins from your kidneys, lymph, lungs, intestines and also your skin. With the kind of poisonous substances and chemicals that are present in the environment today, it is critical to detoxify your body, at least once a year. This is what you have to do:

- *Lighten up your toxic load by eliminating coffee, alcohol, cigarettes, saturated fats and refined sugars that can act as obstacles in your healing process.*
- *Replace your personal Health care products (toothpastes, deodorants, shampoos and cleansers) and chemical-based household cleaners by natural alternatives*
- *Relieve your stress by getting into programs such as Yoga, meditation and Qigong*
- *Include lots of fiber in your diet through brown rice and fresh vegetables and fruits that are grown organically.*
- *Drink lots of water*
- *Adopt a routine with a simple workout, a few breathing exercises and some walking.*

Then vs. Now

What we see on the table now is totally different from what we used to eat when we were growing up.

During those times, there were not too many ads for junk food on TV. There weren't too many restaurants that offered home delivery service. Takeaways were very few. There was no way we could place a food order from a mobile app that said '50% off on the second 'cheese burst pizza.'

We only ate home-cooked - plain but nutritious food. There were times when we did indulge, especially during festivals; yet, there were no toxins in those food items. I hardly ever remember visiting a restaurant during my childhood. The first ever time I ate at a restaurant must be when I was fourteen years of age. The next time I remember I was sixteen.

When we compare ourselves with today's kids, we see them obsessed with food. Most of the foods they crave for have no natural flavors, nor do they contain any nutrition. We spend the whole day in front of our computers, keeping our cell phones to our ears and all we survive on are empty calories that we then wash down with cans of colas. All this is leading us towards a massive Health crisis.

Eat to live; don't live to eat

We cannot live without food; but we have to keep in mind the quality of the food we take and how well-balanced it is. Ultimately, the input has to match the output.

Secret #07: Use it or Lose it!

No one knows your body like you do. Listen to it. It does talk. Let your body be your most trusted personal trainer.

Use it or lose it!

This is exactly what you need to remember. Whether it is Wealth, your brains, some exceptional talent, your habits or even those muscles that you had developed with lot of efforts, when you stop using them, they begin to rot, or atrophy. And once this happens, you may never be able to stop the cycle of self-destruction.

Maintenance is something that everything needs. Your Health needs it too. Once you have achieved a Healthy state of body and mind, you have to put in the same efforts to maintain it. It is important to stick to a routine and develop some habits in order to make sure you live Healthy throughout your life. Even a few days of sluggishness can nullify all your previous efforts.

Secret #07: Use it or Lose it!

Good Health practices increase productivity

Companies today are promoting Healthy lifestyles and encouraging employees to become active, only because absenteeism and their tall medical bills have begun to eat into the company's profits. They have no choice but to incorporate wellness programs into their office regimens. If you are wondering how you can contribute to the Healthy lifestyles of your employees and encourage them to become active and productive, here are a few things you can start with:

Secret #07: Use it or Lose it!

- Providing fresh fruits and vegetable salads for your employees
- Having a nutritious meal plan that keeps your employees Healthy and active
- Offering gym memberships
- Encouraging group workouts
- Investing in ergonomic desk equipment

Give them new challenges to face, help them learn new things and maintain an interesting workplace environment where employees will love to work.

Secret #07: Use it or Lose it!

Early to bed early to rise

Whatever job you might be in, you can adopt a Healthy lifestyle, simply by rising early.

The morning time is called the *'Brahma Muhurtham'* or the golden time of the day. This is when nature is at its optimum - and ready to share its entire positive vibes with you! Try rising up early one morning, at the break of the dawn and gaze around. If you are an observant person, you will notice...

The golden sun rising in the distant horizon....

The chirping birds....

The Gentle Breeze...

Soak it all up and bask in its glory. Take a walk or a jog. Do some exercises, yoga or meditation. It will make you feel energetic, empowered and enriched to spend your day at office. If you happen to lose that one hour early in the morning you will end up searching for it the whole day. You have to use this or you are definitely going to lose it.

You will be surprised to know how many successful people start their day early in the morning.

Margaret Thatcher would wake up at 5 am every day

Secret #07: Use it or Lose it!

4:30 am is the time Robert Iger, the CEO of Disney wakes up everyday

Frank Lloyd Wright, an American writer, architect of repute, would start his day at 4 am

Tim Cook, the CEO of Apple and Michelle Obama, the first lady of USA hit the gym at 5 am in the morning

Anna Wintour of Vogue plays a tennis match, every morning

Richard Branson of Virgin Airlines sticks to his workout routine every day, which makes him gain four hours' worth of extra productivity.

Rising up early in the morning and exercising, takes a lot of discipline. Over time this discipline gives you the power to control things and shape up your destiny. This is the key to achieve success and maintain it.

Here are a few tips from celebrities that might take you a long way towards your success:

- ☑ ***Victoria Beckham,*** *English businesswoman, fashion designer, model and singer, author of Honestly Healthy Cookbook:* Replace refined sugar with honey or coconut palm sugar. Eat raw food as much as possible. Have dairy products made from goat's or sheep's milk. Start your day with a glass of hot water mixed with a tea spoon of lemon juice. This will boost up your alkaline levels.

Secret #07: Use it or Lose it!

- ☑ ***Rihanna***, *Barbadian Singer and song-writer:* Eat five small meals per day instead of 3 large meals. Each of these meals should contain one lean protein, adequate fiber, low-GI carbohydrate, a sugar-free drink and good fats, all totaling up to 300 calories.

- ☑ ***Kristen Bell,*** *American actress and singer:* If you find it hard to schedule your workouts, try to do some activities with your friends. Instead of hitting the movies on Saturday nights, you can go bike riding, hiking with your dogs or even play the Ultimate Frisbee. While being social and lots of fun, this will also give you a good workout.

- ☑ ***Drew Barrymore,*** *American actress, author, director, model and producer:* Whatever you eat, eat a little bit lesser than what you usually eat.

- ☑ ***Valerie Bertinelli***, *American Actress*: Be aware of what you eat and ask yourself why you are eating it. Is it because you are hungry or do you just want to soothe yourself?

Secret #07: Use it or Lose it!

- ☑ ***Jennifer Lopez***, *American actress, singer, author, fashion designer, dancer, and producer*: Eat whatever you want but don't overeat. Avoid eating desserts. If you have to, at least limit yourself.

- ☑ ***Diane Sawyer,*** *American Television Journalist*: It is very important to drink lots of water. You can cut up a few lime slices and put them in your ice cube tray. Add a few lime ice cubes into your glass of water. It tastes so much better than plain water.

- ☑ ***Virginia Madsen,*** *American actress and Producer*: Most people love Popcorn. You can make it with a bit of olive oil to make it Healthier.

Your goal should be to push yourself up to the limit, both physically, as well as, mentally. Increase your endurance levels slowly. Strive for perfection. Very soon you will become mentally sharp and physically strong. Just as ideas are food for the brain, exercise is food for the body. Not only does it activate you physically, it also keeps you mentally energized.

Secret #07: Use it or Lose it!

All said and done, the time to make change is NOW.

Stop that procrastination

Stop doubting

Stop making all self-deluding, lame excuses to yourself - "Sorry! I don't have the time!"

If you have time to abuse your body with a workaholic lifestyle, you certainly have time to repair and replenish your body. You just need to learn to be your own healer, as animals are.

Seen how a pet dog licks his festering wound to Health again?

You don't have to do that; but you can do something even more dramatic to achieve the same results - you have to look after your body. Is that a very tall order?

Slow down………. smell those roses……….listen to a bird's flapping wings; a baby's happy gurgling sound. Make time for that kind of music. Go to the beach, swim in a lake, take a bath, and just unwind. Smell the fresh air, feel the breeze on you face and you will feel fresh as the flower, laden with the morning dew!

Secret #07: Use it or Lose it!

Change the way you fuel your body. No more self-abuse. No more mindless binging on the run. Stop, eat, sleep, forget and relax.

Cut back on fast foods. Make time to have lunch or dinner at home with your family. Pack snacks from home if you can't resist those in-between hunger pangs. Don't pick up the phone to order a pizza.

Get organized! Cut back on caffeine. Switch to organic tea or a glassful of fresh water with half a lemon squeezed in it. It will give you the best immunity against all diseases.

Check out the 'Drink More Water' campaign that's going viral across the media world. Watch their YouTube video.

Secret #07: Use it or Lose it!

Cut out processed foods. They contain refined sugars and preservatives that you know are not good for you. They create cravings for more toxic foods. Instead consume real food. Later, don't forget to exercise and burn the extra calories you consume. Change your sedentary lifestyle. Even if you have to, get up once in a while, stretch and twitch a muscle or two. It will do you a world of good.

Just assume that you invested a huge amount of money to buy a new car. Can you imagine what could happen to it if you fail to service it as per the schedule?

Of course it will begin to rot.

It is the same thing that can happen to your body and to your brain cells too!

Secret #08: Be Different; you don't have to follow the Crowd

You'll learn, as you get older,

that rules are made to be broken.

Be bold enough to live life on your terms,

and never, ever apologize for it.

Go against the grain; refuse to conform.

Take the road less traveled instead of the well-beaten path.

Laugh in the face of adversity, and leap before you look.

Dance as though EVERYBODY is watching.

March to the beat of your own drummer.

And stubbornly refuse to fit in.

— Mandy Hale

Secret #08: Be Different; you don't have to follow the Crowd

Don't Seek Safety in Numbers

Have you seen Apple's Think Different 2013 spot?

Here's the You Tube link -

https://www.youtube.com/watch?v=SswMzUWOiJq

Following the herd when being in one, may make you feel very comfortable and accepted. However, this makes you just another average human being who has no special or extraordinary talents. This can very much come in the way of your success. Therefore, it is necessary to THINK Different ... think away from the group, even if that means getting singled out from the group.

Don't have a herd mentality

I got to realize this when I joined first year of college at the age of eighteen. This was when I began to observe other people's behavior and started seriously thinking about the direction my life was taking.

One day, I was taking an evening stroll with a couple of my friends. They were chatting away but I was lost deep in thoughts. At one point, I told them that I was very disappointed with the world. When they asked me why, I explained to them that I was high on expectations when I joined the campus. However, after spending a few months, I felt I was surrounding by mediocrity and people lacking any real drive or motivation to change their circumstances.

Later I realized that the main reason for this kind of a lethargic attitude was that people are intrinsically resistant to change. In other words, they really don't want to be any different, from anyone else. They just want to blindly follow the herd. They behave exactly in the way others in the group behave. The fear of getting singled out is something that stops them from being different. That's why we have so few inventors, discoverers and entrepreneurs among us.

Secret #08: Be Different; you don't have to follow the Crowd

Entrepreneurs think differently!

Entrepreneurs dare to be different. They do things their way. They thrive on the challenges life throws at them. They trust their instincts and make the right decisions while addressing complex business problems.

Have you watched any of the episodes of Dragon's Den and figured out what drove these dragons to success? More recently did you see Zootopia and the little bunny rabbit's desire to challenge the status quo and wish and train to be a first bunny cop in an idyllic township called Zootopia?

That little bunny had what it takes to realize her most cherished dream.

What does it mean to be different?

Being different implies:

- ☑ Not following the well-trodden path that everyone takes
- ☑ Choosing your own destiny and charting your own course from there
- ☑ Taking extraordinary risks and chances in life
- ☑ Going against the tide and set rules
- ☑ Following one's dreams like an obsessive maniac

Ironically, although each of us is unique in our own way, we work hard to become exactly like everyone else and that's such a pity!

We follow the norms of the society in conforming to all 'common-sense' principles, however against the grain it might be for us.

Therefore, decide for yourself whether you want to be a sheep in a herd or a lone lion in the jungle. Your choice will decide whether you will rule the world, or fade away into the masses.

What stops you from being different?

There are many myths that make us follow the herd. Here are a few:

The group is always right

History may prove otherwise, but we tend to believe that whatever the group thinks is always right. We hold that if a large pool of people believe in a particular idea, it must automatically be correct. We find it hard to get over the fact that the majority can have less knowledge than an individual. In the long-run this kind of a debilitating belief can hurt a person's self-confidence and self-esteem and shake his faith in his own worth.

Shifting from the group can lead one astray

Nothing can be farthest from truth. We believe that it's safer to go with decisions that the group takes because that involves minimum amount of risk-taking. On the flip side, decisions made independently can be counter-productive. But then this is a risk every entrepreneur takes. Indeed, this is the price nine out of ten entrepreneurs pay - so that the tenth one among them can emerge victorious.

Frankly, it's not a huge price to pay. Just imagine: if those nine had resisted paying this price, would we have had any ground-breaking inventions?

That said, it's important to compare two or more set of decisions by analyzing all their pros and cons. In the end, if your individual decision appears correct and ethical, by all means move away from the group.

It is safer to follow the crowd when you are just starting out

Ever since, we came into this world, our parents, our teachers and our college advisors have always directed the course of our life. Then when we step into the real world we get completely befuddled by the limitless options available. We take advice from people whom we respect; yet, the loudest voice that we hear is the roar of the crowd.

Again, it appears easier to go with the crowd when things are so confusing. And that's where things begin to gradually go wrong. You may end up choosing a path that may not be the right one for you. Once you plunge, it may be late in the day to realize your folly, and the reverse course has already closed for you. The result is neither happiness nor success.

Secret #08: Be Different; you don't have to follow the Crowd

Better late than never!

As a kid how many times were you asked - "What do you want to be when you grow up?" My response was always "I want to become successful" and everyone would laugh at my answer.

Later, when I grew up and took a regular job, I realized that my job did not really satisfy me. And it wasn't just the pay, which of course, was miserly. The long working hours, the mechanical nature of the job, the inflexible routine, an imposing boss, daily commuting – everything was taking the job out of my first job. Then one fine day, I gathered enough courage to call it quits.

Now looking back on those turbulent years, I am glad I did what I did, because that was the right option for me.

Learn From People Who Left the Herd

They dared to be different.... So can you!

This is about a speech that **Steve Jobs** gaveat the Stanford Stadium to the graduating class of Stanford. After helping the students draw lessons from his life, he concluded his speech with an advice...

> "You've got to find what you love... The only way to do great work is to love
>
> what you do. If you haven't found it yet, keep looking, and don't settle."

The speech earned him a standing ovation from an audience of 23,000

Sir Arthur Conan Doyle, the author of the Sherlock Holmes series, first started his career as a physician. He practiced for years and realized that writing was his actual passion. Later, he went on to pen 60 stories about the mythical detective, and the rest, as they say, is history. Doyle is dead but Holmes lives on.

Christopher Columbus: He was the one who discovered that the world is round and all he got in return was a lot of mockery.

David Edward Hughes: He is the one who invented the radio. His folks admitted him into a mental hospital when he declared that he could transmit sound frequencies through the air.

Frederick W. Smith: He wrote a paper on 'overnight delivery' when he was a student at Yale University. His professor gave him a "C." This didn't discourage him from starting FedEx, which is now a company that is worth more than two billion dollars

J.K. Rowling: She was a single mom living on welfare. At the age of 31, she started writing the Harry Potter Series from a coffee shop. Today, she is known as the best British Novelist and the series became a super-duper success.

Pejman Nozad: He started out as a Rug dealer. Today he is counted among the most successful angel investors of the Silicon Valley.

Harrison Ford: It was as a carpenter that he started his career. Today, he has achieved a lot of fame as an actor and producer.

Suze Orman: Working as a waitress till 30 years of age, she went on to become a finance guru, a motivational speaker and a best-selling author.

Mark Cuban, a successful entrepreneur and a billionaire: Working as a bartender in his own bar until the age of 25, he went on to become the owner of Dallas Mavericks.

And there are many more!

There wasn't any fixed pattern that these innovators and creative people followed. They tried out various things and in the end hit the jackpot. In their own unique ways, and with their brilliant ideas, they changed the world.

Most of these successful people were initially mocked at, ridiculed and singled-out. People stared at them and whispered about them. Yet, all this did not stop them from breaking from their herd. If they hadn't, we would have never been able to benefit from their companies, their inventions or their insights.

While many lead the lives of the sheep, being beaten down by authority year after year, there are some that decide to be the wolves. These are the stubborn trouble makers who go with their own ideas of how they want the things to be. They stand out from the crowd, create waves and even manage to annoy a lot of people. Yet, they are the ones who achieve happiness and success.

They make their own plans, follow their own dreams and find great happiness!

They make sure their lives are exactly how they want them to be.

Secret #08: *Be Different; you don't have to follow the Crowd*

A Wolf is someone who trusts his own desires. He gets things done his own way. He ignores everybody who comes in the way.

Unfortunately, every wolf will have to pay a price for ignoring everyone…..

He becomes lonely and separated from the herd of sheep he used to belong to!

Yet, he receives a great reward for having that faith in himself……..

Happiness, Success and lots of money!

Once you get into the habit of using your own brain, following your own passions and tapping your own intuitions, you will be ready to reach greater heights of success!

Secret #09: Explore your Options before you Jump

Breaking from the herd leaves you with limitless options......

It is great to explore these options before jumping into what seems to be the right option for you!

Unless you try out different paths in life it is difficult to stumble upon the perfect road that's been carved only for you. Be flexible. Try out different ways. If they turn out to be wrong, eliminate them from your options. If one turns out right, consider yourself lucky and stick to it.

Go start a business if you are considering entrepreneurship.....

Get into internship if you want to enter the corporate world....

Go for it right away! Do not wait.

If you do not like it later, there is always the option of re-aligning your path.

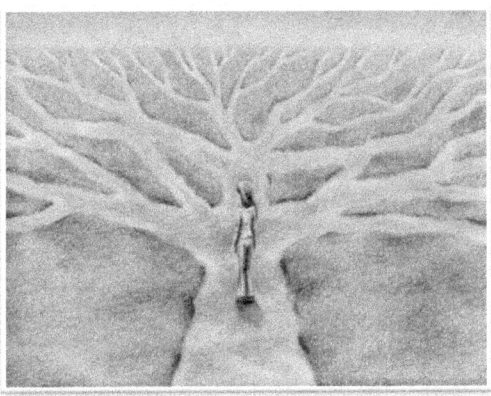

Secret #09: Explore your Options before you Jump

Self-Assessment

There are four attributes that will help you zero in on your perfect career:

- *Values*
- *Interests*
- *Personality Traits*
- *Skills*

Answers to the following questions might help you in choosing a path that you may like:

- *Who am I and who do I want to be?*
- *What are the most important goals in my life?*
- *What are the values that guide me?*
- *What are the ideas that excite me?*
- *What are the activities that I find most engaging?*
- *What are the skills and talents that I possess?*
- *What am I good at?*
- *What are the assets that my experiences have helped me gain?*

Secret #09: Explore your Options before you Jump

- *What is the kind of knowledge and skills I need to develop for my personal as well as professional growth?*
- *What do I have to do to create new opportunities and make things happen?*

Explore and you shall find

Once you have determined your top V.I.P.S. (Values, interests, personality traits and skills), the next step is to short list your career / job options.

Don't bother about the pecking order when you are drawing up this wish list.

Once you have the wish list ready, match it with your self-assessment sheet. This will help you understand where you need to set your priorities and conserve your energies. Your goal should be to understand where your interests lie and what opportunities are available to match those interests.

Secret #09: Explore your Options before you Jump

You can follow this three-step method to find out what interests you in life:

- *Research and Study*
- *Networking and Interviewing*
- *Evaluation and Decision-Making*

This process may appear a little boring and time-consuming at first; but believe me, it will help you face your fears head-on, take few chances and make complicated decisions. Finally, it will help you make a deliberate and strategic plan for yourself.

Do whatever you like to do; but focus on the future because that is where you are going to live all your life!

Almost every single day at least one person breaks himself from the herd. When are you planning to do it?

When will you be transformed into a thinker from a follower?

It is not going to be easy. People may make fun of you; but it shouldn't bother you.

What matters is your goal... your dream... your passion.

Secret #09: Explore your Options before you Jump

You may be inspired by the success stories of other people you have heard of. Now it's time to inspire others with your story.

Herd mentality is often a hard mentality

It's difficult to soften it. You need a lot of strength to resist all those collective challenges to break away from the herd. It means going against the popular beliefs and notions that have always been a part of your life. However you need to remember that just because a crowd consists of many people it doesn't become wiser. Have you heard about the Pied Piper story? You may end up falling off the cliff by getting led by the crowd. If that is not where you want to be, take the following steps:

Secret #09: Explore your Options before you Jump

Be aware: Don't just believe what is being told to you. Try to look for facts. Critically analyze the statements. Don't keep doing something because you have been doing it for ages now. It is time to break away from your routine and change. Else, you will be left being just a copy of the others in the herd.

Experiment: Determine your own likes and dislikes, without going with the opinions of others. Do not mimic others like sheep. When you go to a restaurant with your friends, order something that you want to eat or drink. Don't just order the same items that your friends order. Same when you have to choose a career. Don't go with the choices of others. Find out what your interests are and where your skills lie. It is okay to experiment.

Take your time: Making up your mind or selecting an option from many could take quite some time. Hurrying may not really help. Many might make their choices in a hurry. You don't have to. Take your time; analyze things; compare your choices and then come up with the right decision.

Secret #09: Explore your Options before you Jump

Stand out: Be different. Stand out from the crowd. Ignore the comments that you hear from other people. Forget what they think about you. It is people of low self-esteem that tend to copy others, only to be accepted by the society. What is more important is to achieve your goal and make your folks be proud of you. They might ridicule you today; but tomorrow when you are successful, they will respect you and maybe even follow your footsteps.

You will never become an innovator, a leader or a successful entrepreneur if you keep doing what others are doing. Following the crowd is probably the worst way to live. Do what you want to do... not for others... but for yourself... for your own happiness. Success will be yours soon!

Secret #10: Find Fulfilment in your Life and Work

> *The more intensely we feel about an idea or a goal, the more assuredly the idea, buried deep in our subconscious, will direct us along the path to its fulfillment.*
>
> —Earl Nightingale

> *Don't just climb the mountain because it's there. Really think about whether that's the mountain you want to climb*
>
> — Kim Smith

Do you remember that excitement you felt when you opened up your Birthday gift and found exactly what you wished for?

Did you ever rescue someone in need and felt overjoyed at their expression of gratitude?

This is the kind of fulfillment I am talking about here. Yet, it differs from person to person. What seems fulfilling to me may not feel so rewarding to you and vice versa.

For instance, I might find absolute contentment in living the life of a minimalist with a 9to5 job, a short nap on the couch and a cold brewski to end my day.

Keeping the house clean and planning a trip to the hills may bring contentment to someone else.

However, these may mean nothing to you.

A simple and fulfilling life is one where you work to live and not live to work.

Taking care of yourself and your own, without paying heed to what is going on in the world, is contentment!

You can find fulfillment in any thing you do, if you put your heart, mind and soul into it. It's called living in the moment. It is important to be yourself and not be bothered about always conforming to the established norms. However, keeping this kind of attitude requires a lot of focus and, of course courage too.

Highly-fulfilled people are often the most beautiful and the most successful ones in this world. They possess a special energy that attracts other good people and good things to them. They shine wherever they are. On the flip side, not all successful, beautiful people are highly fulfilled in life.

Choose the life you want to live

You need to make your own choices in your life, be it good ones, bad ones, happy ones, unhappy ones, purposeful ones or void ones. You have to seek your own fulfillment and happiness in life, despite the circumstances and despite the people who appear to try to snatch it away from you. I feel it's important to make your own decisions that reflect who you are and what you believe in. Living up to the beliefs and standards that other people have set for you, will never lead you to fulfillment or happiness.

Secret #10: Find Fulfilment in your Life and Work

Fulfillment is not always about achieving goals

Achieving your goals or winning may not always bring you satisfaction. Sometimes it might even bring you disappointment because you have nowhere else to go.

This is just like the guy whose main aim in life was to climb a particular mountain. However, once he did that, he was very disappointed because his goal in life had ended right there and yet there was something missing.

A professional football player, I am certain, feels the same after winning the Super Bowl.

I had a similar experience when I was at the University. By the time I completed my senior year, I had done everything that was supposed to give me fulfillment....

I partied to my heart's content .....

Achieved decent grades.....

Spent some quality time with a few attractive girls....

Yet, there was something missing.

I was not fulfilled.

So then, how do you achieve fulfillment in your life and work?

Try to recognize those walls beyond the walls that you have painted....

Have compassion for the voice, irrespective of the language it speaks.....

Be true to yourself, even if it is painful....

Here are four steps that you can follow on a daily basis to achieve happiness, success and fulfillment:

Visualize your goal

This includes visualizing the path that brought you here from where you were and the path that is going to take you where you want to go. It will help you come up with the perfect plan to achieve your goals. It will also stop you from repeating the mistakes that you committed previously.

Secret #10: Find Fulfilment in your Life and Work

Assume responsibility for your actions

Assuming responsibility for your deeds shows maturity. Most of us end up blaming others for our failures and opportunities missed in life. Being responsible will earn you others' respect, even if you fail. People around will start trusting you. They will begin to show confidence in your decisions and abilities.

Keep learning

Learning is something that never stops, if you have the right bend of mind. I am not talking only about formal education here; but about the process of life itself. Always have an open mind and accept life as it comes. Learn newer ways of doing things. In today's world, change is the only thing that is constant; and if you are a wise person, you will try to embrace this change instead of fighting against it.

Take time to appreciate

How often do you say the magical words "Thank you" every time someone does a favor to you? Be thankful for the wonderful opportunities and challenges that come your way. This will change your perspective towards life and motivate you to achieve more, with your optimism.

Secret #10: Find Fulfilment in your Life and Work

Life is not about reaching that gold at the end of the rainbow. Your life itself should become that rainbow, within which you should live every day.

Clear the inner fog that is blocking your vision.

Fulfillment differs from person to person. It is something that is intensely personal. You need to look into yourself and see who you are and what life means to you.

As poet William Blake said, "Cleanse the doors of perception."

I find this phase of my life most exciting. As I pen this section of my book I am beginning to take pride in my achievement as a life entrepreneur. I believe it's just the beginning. You can become an entrepreneur, irrespective of your age and profession. Just set your priorities straight.

Secret #10: Find Fulfilment in your Life and Work

So here is the question.....

Is your life leading you to fulfillment?

Answer the following questions with a Yes or No:

- Does your career or work seem energizing to you?
- Are you a happily married /happily single person?
- Are you at peace with the people in your life?
- Do have close friends with whom you can be at ease?
- Is your work a fulfilling part of your life?
- Are you at peace with God?
- Are your debts and obligations under your control?
- Do you do things that you totally enjoy, in your leisure time?
- Do you take pleasure in simple things of your life?
- Do you look forward to start a new day of your life?
- Have you saved enough money to have fun in life?
- Do people respect you for what you are and accept your wants and needs?
- Have you determined your goals and are you progressing towards achieving them?
- Are your personal needs satisfied to the maximum extent?
- Can you get things done in an easy and a convenient way?
- Is your life oriented around your personal values?
- Do you feel happy every time you walk into your home?

Secret #10: Find Fulfilment in your Life and Work

- Are you taking good care of yourself?
- Are you living life your way?
- Do you do any activities to manage stress effectively?
- Do you manage to spend some time for yourself during the day?
- Is your life free of regrets?

If you have answered with a 'Yes' to all of the above questions you are completely fulfilled in your life. If not, you have to work towards this goal. The secret mantra will begin to dawn on you as you finish reading this chapter.

Have you ever wondered why you are here.... what you are supposed to do with your life... and what exactly is the point of all this?

I have too.

This was when I was 17 years old. I happened to read a quote:

"If you live each day as if it was your last, someday you'll most certainly be right."

The line made a deep impression on me and ever since I have been asking myself -how would I lead my life if this was my last day on the planet?

Secret #10: Find Fulfilment in your Life and Work

If you are really honest with yourself, you will probably realize two things in life:

1. Where you are now in life?
2. What has to be done from here?

The answer to the first question might bruise your ego and make you feel uncomfortable. The second might make you sacrifice many things that may be close to your heart. This is definitely not easy; but if you fail to face this challenge, nothing is going to change in your life.

After giving six years of my life to establish a business, I gave it all up to come up with something better. It was a major decision; but I wish I had taken it earlier.

Often in the path of life, there comes a time when you get stuck in the daily grind. When you do not find the courage or the inspiration to move on, to remain still and examine life. However, the various life paths laid out in front of you might seem scary when it comes to taking a long-term decision.

You don't know what to do. You feel absolutely hopeless and directionless. This is the time when you have to take the plunge. If not, your life will remain stuck in the rut.

You might be unfamiliar with the path…

things might not go as predicted…

yet with time, you will learn to adapt and grow.

The plan that you embark upon may not appear perfect at first…

but somewhere down the line, it will begin to fit in, if you keep trying.

You will feel alive again, despite the uncertainties that surround you.

There is no perfect way to live

Passions, ambitions, priorities and differences differ from person to person and so does the concept of a perfect life. Yet, we all look for a life that is meaningful and purposeful. This meaning and purpose may also differ from person to person.

What is most important is to keep an open mind as you move forward. No matter what path you choose and what you decide to do, you should not live to regret your choices. Find out what matters the most to you and pursue that dream with passion and purpose.

This story of Adam Steltzner, the NASA scientist, may inspire you in this direction:

Secret #10: Find Fulfilment in your Life and Work

Adam Steltzner headed the team that worked on Mars Rover's successful landing. Once he revealed in an NPR interview that he was part of a rock band. All his friends joined college, while he still waited for his stardom. One night, when he was on his way home from a gig, he happened to look up at the stars and got so completely fascinated by the Orion constellation. He decided at that moment of divine intervention that he had to work towards understanding the laws that govern the universe. That's when he enrolled himself in a physics course, which then led him to complete his Ph.D.and brought him to where he is today.

We all nurture our cherished dreams. However, not all of us go full-throttle after our dreams. We get stuck somewhere on the way, without knowing where to go from there. This is what you need to do in order to live the life of your dreams:

Secret #10: Find Fulfilment in your Life and Work

- ☑ Find out why you got stuck. See what you need to do in order to move forward. Sometimes it is important to look back in order to move forward.

- ☑ Stop making lame excuses if you wish to move forward. Excuses mask fear. It's important to transform fears into faith.

- ☑ Live in the present.

- ☑ Every human being in this world comes endowed with hidden talents. You must have yours too. It is important to recognize them and make the most of those talents to get where you want to go.

- ☑ Do not settle down in life? Don't. Take risk to break the status quo and learn newer and better ways of doing things.

Secret #11: Live in Tune with Your True Self

> *He who lives in harmony with himself lives in harmony with the world*
>
> - Marcus Aurelius

People who live life on their own terms always inspire me. They dare to take the road less travelled. They discover the purpose of their lives and pursue it with a doggedness that never ceases to surprise me. There is a poem that I am reminded of here. "The Road not Taken" by Robert Frost:

Two roads diverged in a yellow wood,

And sorry I could not travel both

And be one traveler, long I stood

And looked down one as far as I could

To where it bent in the undergrowth;

Then took the other, as just as fair,

And having perhaps the better claim,

Because it was grassy and wanted wear;

Though as for that the passing there

Had worn them really about the same,

And both that morning equally lay

In leaves no step had trodden black.

Oh, I kept the first for another day!

Yet knowing how way leads on to way,

I doubted if I should ever come back.

I shall be telling this with a sigh

Somewhere ages and ages hence:

Two roads diverged in a wood, and I—

I took the one less traveled by,

And that has made all the difference.

Secret #11: Live in Tune with Your True Self

When you want something desperately, you need to find out why you want it before you go there and get it

You may wish to own a fancy car only to feel special; but once you have it, you may realize that you need an upgraded model

You may desire to start up a business in order to make money; but it may still leave you as unfulfilled as you were

You may put in a lot of efforts to lose that ten pounds and look sexier; yet you may not get any kind of reinforcement from that special person in your life

Have you ever wondered why you never attain fulfillment in spite of achieving your goals?

This is mainly because your inner self is not aligned with your outer self. It is because you are not at peace with yourself. Whatever you do in life, it is important to live in tune with yourself. Else, you end up getting stressed, confused and may be even sick.

For some of us, security brings peace of mind….

For a few others peace is about clearing your life off the clutter and finding calmness ….

Secret #11: Live in Tune with Your True Self

Many others feel being in peace is all about accepting and letting go…

However, peace is about everything you do.

You need to behave with integrity at all times to feel peace within yourself.

Life is never a bed of roses. Things may not always turn out the way you expect them to. People and circumstances may prevent you from doing things the way you want to. Yet you need to hang on to that integrity, irrespective of the kind of challenges you encounter. If you can do this, you will be able to sleep peacefully and with a clear conscience even when circumstances around you are challenging.

Here are a few tips that can help you develop that kind of peace within yourself:

1. Determine your "ideal self."

By ideal self I mean the person you wish to be in life. Prepare a list of qualities that you want to cultivate within yourself, such as kindness, tolerance, patience, dignity and so on. Determine how you want to respond to difficult situations in life. Check out the principles that you want to uphold in life.

2. If you cannot take the perfect action, do the next right thing that strikes you

It is not always possible to take the perfect action in life. A lot depends on your physical and mental state, the understanding you have of the situation, and the obstacles that you face and so on. What is important is to stick to your principles and do the next right thing that comes to your mind.

3. Quit being a perfectionist

Sometimes, perfectionism can create unnecessary complications in life. Not everything in life needs to be picture perfect. Sometimes, you need to take it easy and keep things simple. You often end up flogging yourself, making yourself feel absolutely miserable or get mad at yourself to make appear absolutely perfect. All this is not really necessary. You can still make progress even while being imperfect.

4. Correct your mistakes immediately

It is human to err. In your effort to achieve your goals you might end up doing something wrong, acting mean or treating someone in an unfair way. Once you realize this, apologize or correct your mistake immediately. This way, you will rid yourself of the guilt and be at peace with yourself and your world.

5. Be patient

Not everyone can be like you or live up to your expectations. When someone tries to push those buttons, take a deep breath before you react.

6. Live and let live

Always try to maintain a positive outlook. Make efforts to understand people instead of judging them. Forgiving others is for your own good. Be compassionate. By doing so you will not only be helping others, you will also be enhancing your self-esteem.

Secret #11: Live in Tune with Your True Self

7. Think before you act

When you are angry or frustrated it's quite common to lose your temper. However, before you pre-judge or respond, think about how you will feel later on. Is this going to make you happy? Will you get back your peace of mind by doing so? If NO is the answer you get, it is better to stay quiet.

8. Summarize your actions and validate yourself

Make it a point to take stock of all your actions before you wind up your day. Check if you have taken efforts to maintain your integrity while dealing with situations. Find out where you went wrong and take measures to correct those. Make sure you don't repeat those mistakes again.

Once you are at peace with yourself, you'll be at peace with the world around you. From that point onwards, you'll start making progress and achieve all your goals without any setbacks.

Secret #11: Live in Tune with Your True Self

As a child, I loved to write stories. For hours I would sit in my room and write about aliens, superheroes, great warriors and spin yarns about my friends and family members. It was not that I wanted people to read them. I never wished to impress my teachers or parents through my stories. I wrote them because I felt happy writing. However, after a while, I totally stopped writing. If you ask me why, I don't even remember the reason.

It was in my mid-twenties that I realized writing was my passion. Yet, I had my own reasons back then, not to reconnect with this passion. If ever my eight-year old self would happen to ask my 20-year old self, why I stopped writing… I would have probably said…

Secret #11: Live in Tune with Your True Self

"I am not really that gooda writer"

Or *"I don't think anyone would read what I write"*

Or maybe *"writing cannot fetch me this kind of money."*

These answers would have made my eight-year old self start crying. Nevertheless, I am happy I did reconnect with my passion although I started a little later. Writing has given me the satisfaction that nothing else ever gave.

Nothing compares with the feeling of doing what you love doing. As children, we all liked to indulge in activities that we were absolutely passionate about. Some of us loved our art, writing inspired a few, it was music for a couple of others and then there was photography, traveling or even helping others. Making time for these activities gave us absolute happiness then. However, as we grew up, we got so busy with our mundane study activities, career pursuits, work and family that we forgot what our original passion was.

Has this happened to you?

It is not too late. You can still reconnect with your past passion. All you need to do is make up your mind and take some time out in pursuit of your passion.

Reconnecting with your passion

Passion is not only for those who have a lot of time at hand and no responsibilities in life. Passion is for people who want to be happy in life. Passion provides an outlet to escape. It acts as a medium to express your deepest emotions. It helps you distract yourself from the mundane things of life. It changes the way you see yourself, your loved ones and the world around you.

Pursuing your passion is like meditation that helps you relax. It is an excellent stress-buster that gives you instant happiness. Not just does it boost your emotional well-being, it also improves your physical health.

When you follow a creative hobby or passion, you tend to be more creative, collaborative and even helpful at work. It can help you in:

- Developing new skills
- Grasping knowledge
- Enhancing your awareness of your strengths and weaknesses
- Challenging conventional thinking
- Sparking up your creative instinct

Not just this; passion even helps you tide over the grief of losing a loved one. If you still feel that you don't have the time to pursue your hobby or a passion, think again. There are many celebrities and successful people who took the time to pursue their passions. Seek inspiration from them:

- Millionaire Warren Buffet takes time from his busy schedule to play Ukulele
- Albert Einstein, the famous scientist and inventor, would play his violin and enjoyed sailing
- Bill Gates, the Founder of Microsoft, does not always lead an online life. He loves to collect rare books.
- Thomas Alva Edison, the famous inventor, was a huge follower of fad diets.
- If you have ever visited Disney Land you may not be surprised if I tell you that Walt Disney adored model trains.

Re-visit the rules you have set for yourself

We often tend to imbibe 'I Can't' and 'This is not the right time' rules from others, without thinking of whether they would make sense in our lives. Instead, we should create new rules based on our experiences in life. In order to reconnect with your passion you may have to break some of the old, conditional rules that seem unnecessary or too rigid, and figure out your way forward.

Secret #11: Live in Tune with Your True Self

Make a list of things you love

Jot down the activities that you love to do in your leisure time and then select the top three hobbies. Spend about a minute visualizing these. It could be art, writing, singing or power yoga. See how it energizes you and elevates your mood. Check if it brings contentment. If it does, this is the passion you should reconnect with.

Seek others who get it

All your life you have been surrounded by people who have no time to pursue their passion. How would you feel to be surrounded by people who share your passion? If you cannot physically connect with such people, you can at least read about them. For instance, if writing is your passion, you can get to know authors or aspiring writers and see how they have pursued their passion. There are many who have turned their passion into a profession and are leading happy lives.

Set out time to nurture your passion

Keep aside at least half an hour each day, or at least about ten minutes per week to nurture your passion. Make space for it in your diary. Once it slips into your routine, try increasing this time gradually, one step at a time.

Introspect if you want to reconnect with your passion. This implies diving deep into your life to understand who you are. Then you have to pull out all the pieces so as to assemble the puzzle of your purpose. Passion is that golden thread that some see as their career or profession, while for others it is a form of expression – their reason for being on this planet.

There is just one more thing I would like to quote here. This is a part of a dialogue that I find very interesting. It is from my favorite movie – *Star Wars*. It says....

"Do or Do not; there is no try"

Playing to Your Talents

You must be familiar with the story of David and Goliath from the Bible. If not, let me help you recall:

David was a shepherd boy who had utmost faith in God. His brothers were all soldiers in the army; but he was not as strong or mighty as them. His father, who was aware of this, put him on the duty of looking after the sheep. At times his brothers would make fun of David; but he gradually learnt to ignore them. He sincerely believed that God was with him always.

He started making use of a sling to drive away the animals when they made attempts to attack his sheep. With practice, he went on to become an expert at using the sling. On a few occasions he was able to save himself and his sheep from a lion and even a bear.

Once when his country was attacked by the enemies, there was a giant in the enemy called Goliath, of whom all the soldiers were scared. David's brothers too were afraid. While everyone thought Goliath was too big a giant to fight against, David thought that Goliath was just too big to miss. Much to everybody's surprise, David was successful in knocking down the giant through his unique talent.

No talent goes waste!

All of us are born with our own unique talents. These are given to us to fulfill some purpose in life. This is what we need to realize and work towards.

Talent is not an activity; it is a personal trait that can become your strength

For instance, if you are a person who minutely analyzes experiences, this could in fact be your talent that you can apply productively, especially when you are involved in front-end initiatives and projects.

Secret #11: Live in Tune with Your True Self

If you love to meet people and establish useful connections and business networks, this talent can emerge to be your key strength, especially if you are in a sales position.

Unless you put your natural talents to use, they may fade out

It's not enough to spot your talent. You also need to find out what you are great at. This changes the game completely.

If you need to succeed in life by capitalizing on who you truly are, you have to recognize your unique talents and find an outlet for their expression. It might take some time; but at the end, it will be worth your while.

Here are a few ways through which you can recognize your talents:

1. Check out what makes you feel strong

This could be a physical or a mental activity. This is something you do repeatedly or think about many times during the day. This is something that energizes you. When you are doing an activity, see which part of it you enjoy the most. Look for patterns where you are constantly thinking about or doing something, almost to the extent of annoying people around you.

2. See where your money is going

This should tell you where your talents lie. For instance, if you spend a lot of money on buying books, your talent lies in seeking or exploring knowledge. In case you are spending a lot on friends, your talent probably lies in communication and in building relationships. I used to spend a lot on buying books and CDs pertaining to personality development.

3. Ask others about your strong points

People around you are in the best position to judge you. They can describe your winning traits and characteristics. You can ask your family members, your friends and your colleagues to find out what they love about you. You will not only be able to identify your strong talents, you will also be in a position to boost your self-confidence. It will help you look at yourself from other peoples' perspective.

If you are an employer you need to be able to recognize and utilize the talents of others to improve their productivity and increase your revenues. In fact recognizing talents is something you need to do from a very young age. It will come of use later in life, if you benchmark your progress against where you were ten years ago, then five years ago, and so on

Retirement is when you stop living at work and start working at living!

After 9 years of working hard and struggling I decided to retire at 31. Retirement to me is not a life where you just sit on your easy chair all day, doing crosswords, reading newspapers, and maybe watching some TV. It was about living life, my terms. It was about not having to worry about making ends meet. It's also about the Financial Freedom.

I still had my businesses going; but I had an excellent team in place to take care of them in my absence….

No more do I have to work hard for money; but I made sure my money was and will be working hard for me….

I have still a long way to become one of the richest men in the world; but I know I don't have to live in poverty anymore….

I have achieved what I wanted to; but I still dream big….

My idol in life is Robert Kiyosaki and he became my Idol ever since I read his book "Rich Dad Poor Dad." I wanted to be a successful businessman ever since then and I am glad I achieved it! Now I want to help you make your dreams come true, which is why I decided to write this book.

Secret #12: Retire While you are Still Young

Ever Since I have retired, I have learnt to enjoy life as it is. I am in perfect health and I have learnt how to maintain it. I spend not just quality but also quantity time with my family. I do what I want and the way I want. I have developed excellent health habits like having lunch before 12 Noon and having dinner before 7 PM. I have successfully stopped watching the TV.

I start my day early and do Yoga with my family….

I make sure everyone in my family keeps fit…..

I am free from stress and tensions…..

I love what I do and give it my 100%.....

I have learnt that Life is beautiful if I know how to live on my terms and THAT is exactly what I am doing now!

Why Retire Young?

If you ask why retire young when you can work till you are 60, I would say why not!

There are many who think they can work till they drop. Most never want to retire unless they are too sick. I say what is the point in retiring when you are too sick?

Secret #12: Retire While you are Still Young

Can you take those exotic vacations that you always wanted to, when you are so sick?

Can you be happy and make everyone around you feel happy?

Of course Not!

When you are so sick, forget taking care of others, you would need someone to take care of you.

The sickness would have made your life miserable and in turn you would be bringing in miseries to the lives of those people who would be serving you.

You are just going to kill the entire purpose of retirement

The best way is to retire when you are still young. This helps you enjoy life and live it the way you want.

You may be thinking that retiring early is something only celebrities, lottery winners, tech tycoons and trust-fund babies can manage. You are wrong! You can too. All you need to do is plan up well, set your goals, carve out a road map and go ahead!

Today you can find many young retirees who come from different walks of life. They were not born rich; they were not celebrities and they did not win lotteries. Some of these people were school teachers, some were writers, some were those who built careers in engineering and finance, a few were entrepreneurs and the others were just like you who were working at their 9-to-5 jobs. Yet they all adopted a mindset that took them towards their goal.

There are many things that we can learn from the kind of lives they leaded and here are a few of those:

They learnt how to be financially independent

You may think that you need to earn a set amount of income before you think of retiring. However, while doing so you fall prey to taxes that consume most of your income. Young retirees do not think this way. For them, it is not the income that counts; it is their savings. They make it a point to save a fixed percentage of their take-home pay. This is when you will feel retirement is very much achievable. A higher income definitely helps but a higher savings percentage would be the key to early retirement.

They believed in spending less; but they were happy

There is a thin line between needs and wants that you need to understand if you want to retire early. It is only when you start comparing yourself with others or fall prey to advertisements that you start spending money on your "wants." Although young retirees spend way below their means, they never view this as a sacrifice. Actually they are perfectly content and even proud of their minimized consumption. You will have to adopt this attitude if you wish to retire young.

They begin to invest early and do it over decades

There are no investing secrets that young retires have access to. They love to keep things simple. They know it takes longer for compound interest to start working its magic. They do exactly what you do; but they start way early than you and keep it going for decades rather than years or months.

They hate paying up high investment fees

Early retirees plan their investments carefully. They do not go for investment vehicles that would require high fees. Looking to banks for investment advice may not be a wise move as most banks are into funds that come with exorbitant fees. A better way is to go with a Robo-advisor that makes use of algorithms to create investor portfolios. This can help you manage sophisticated investments at low-cost

They purchase assets that bring in the cash-flow

It is very important to diversify your portfolio if you want a steady source of income that supports early retirement. Investing in Real-estate is one of the most popular types of alternate investments. However, you cannot just buy a property and wait for it to increase in value. You will have to follow the 1 percent rule of thumb. The gross monthly rent that you get from the real estate property that you buy should amount to at least 1% of its cost price.

Alternatively, you could even go for one of the income-producing websites or ecommerce that are gaining popularity these days. You can expect an annualized return of anywhere between 33 and 50 percent from such sites. However, it is very important that you get some hands-on experience before you go there and start acquiring websites. You have to put in hours of study to understand digital business models and do your research.

It is not easy to retire early; but it is definitely not impossible if you adopt the right mindset and strategy.

PS: Await my next book on "how I retired at 31, healthy and wealthy" to understand the right steps you need to take in order to retire young

Secret #12: Retire While you are Still Young

Key Take Aways

- ☑ Dive into the moment to uncover the path in your life
- ☑ Let go of any expectations, assumptions or external programming
- ☑ Make sure you have everything you require, to take your next step
- ☑ Don't be in a hurry. Don't put in your resignation only because you want to be famous or successful. Accept your situation
- ☑ Make maximum utilization of your available resources
- ☑ Do what makes you feel alive, excited, magnetic and fascinated
- ☑ Give a start to your journey with an open mind
- ☑ Live life as per your unique purpose
- ☑ Stick to your principles and do what seems right to you

All the Best!

www.ingramcontent.com/pod-product-compliance
Lightning Source LLC
Chambersburg PA
CBHW070251190526
45169CB00001B/367